# A Huguenot Family
## 1536-1889

# A HUGUENOT FAMILY

## DES BOUVERIE, BOUVERIE, PLEYDELL-BOUVERIE

## 1536-1889

### by Jacob Radnor

FOXBURY PRESS

The endpaper is taken from a drawing of Longford Castle in 1592
and the title-page from a painting by Marcus May

First published in 2001 by Foxbury Press, 1 Step Terrace, Winchester SO22 5BW

A CIP catalogue record for this book is available from the British Library

ISBN 0-946053-05-7

Designed by Gillian Greenwood

Printed in Great Britain by B.A.S. Printers, Over Wallop, Hampshire

# Contents

# List of portrait paintings

*To my sisters Jane and Harriot*
*and my wife Jill*

# Author's note

These brief notes seem suitable for a short history. The brevity of the book belies the huge amount of work and research that Nancy Steele accomplished. Without her help this tale would never have been told.

I owe thanks, too, to Emma Monson, my son, Peter Pleydell-Bouverie, and Robert Cross for reading the manuscript, and making helpful suggestions. My son, William Folkestone, kindly provided me with his photograph of Longford Castle and Patrick White that of 4 Bouverie Street. I am grateful, too, to Derek Parker for taking a number of photographs of various manuscripts that occur in the book. Jane Cunningham, Melanie Blake and Catherine Wyatt of the Courtauld Institute were responsible for all the colour photography, and some of the black and white illustrations. To them I am deeply indebted.

For help sifting through archive material, I must thank John d'Arcy and Stephen Hobbs, county archivists for Wiltshire and Swindon. Their knowledge was invaluable.

I am grateful to Shione Carden for her work on the family tree.

Finally, I must pay tribute to Heather Purvis for her patience in helping produce and note everything that was necessary for this slim volume.

The story itself is intended to be factual, and I hope it is, although on occasions I have used descriptive stories hoping that the person so described will better reveal his or her character to the reader.

My sisters, and my wife Jill, have often asked where we came from. It certainly wasn't from under a gooseberry bush, and so here is an attempt to describe very briefly the course of events.

*Laurens Des Bouverie*
(Flemish School)

# CHAPTER I

# *Laurens Des Bouverie 1536-1610*

The Bouverie family descend from Laurens Des Bouverie, who was born, so far as is known, in St Jean de Melantois, a small town near Lille. His father was probably a fairly well-to-do but modest landowner. Had he been in England, he might have been the village squire. Laurens' date of birth is not known with certainty, but 1536 is written on a small picture of him hanging at Longford Castle. The picture is of a gentle bearded man. He must, though, have possessed great strength of character, as subsequent events will show.

The district in which the Des Bouveries lived was French-speaking, and was ceded eventually to France under the Treaty of Aix-La-Chapelle, which signified the end of the War of the Austrian Succession. At the time of this narrative, though, it was part of the Spanish Netherlands.

Years after Laurens' birth both the first and second Earls of Radnor went to great pains to find out the whereabouts of Laurens' home, but they failed. A certain amount of time had passed, and it is probable that the rest of the family had dispersed. Some of the family, it is known, went to Holland.

During Laurens' youth the Reformation in Europe was steadily gaining strength. In Geneva Calvin was organising a Reformed Church, which was to have a huge influence throughout Europe. In 1559 he founded an academy to which both ministers and laymen came, so that they could learn about the new religion, and equip themselves to spread its message.

At Longford[1] there is a small painting of Calvin. It is possibly the only painting of him in this country. He was a rather ugly man to look at, and some infer that the same adjective could be applied to his character.

[1] Longford Castle, which became the Bouverie home in 1717

The growth of the Protestant religion in the Low Countries did not please King Philip II of Spain. His reaction was to send the Duke of Alva to the Netherlands to deal with those tempted away from Roman Catholicism to the 'new' religion. It was a period of severe repression. It was against this background that a distressing event took place within the Des Bouverie family.

It is recorded at Longford that Laurens' father accused his son of 'talking too much with his heretic tenants', and also that he 'had not been attending Mass on Sundays'.

Amazingly, he told Laurens that if he did not mend his ways, or if he did not attend Mass on the following Sunday, he would report him to the Inquisition.

This was a very serious threat for a father to direct at his son. The cruelties of the Inquisition are well known and well documented. If an offender recanted fully and speedily, then an admonition and a fine might be the only punishments meted out. Failure to recant would inevitably lead to torture. If under torture the perceived religious deviant still refused to recant, then death by burning at the stake was the final punishment.

Already a friend of Laurens had suffered such a fate. Unprepared to recant he was finally burnt at the stake, dragged there by his own coach horses. A cousin, who thought better of his original decision to embrace the new religion, was merely fined and given a good lecture on the stupidity of his ways.

Laurens, realising that his father's threat was not a hollow one, and that he was in real danger, decided to leave home as quickly as possible. The strength of his feelings towards the new religion outweighed his regard for his father which, in the circumstances, was not surprising. As it turned out, cutting all family ties for ever, he travelled to Frankfurt. By what means he achieved this journey can only be conjectured. Possibly he walked, accepting a lift or two on the way. The distance, though considerable, is not huge. It is obvious, though, from records that he arrived safely, but tired and dispirited.

So far as Laurens was concerned, Frankfurt represented a safe haven from the persecution with which he had been threatened. It was a city state and one of the centres of the Reformation. Calvin himself often spent time there. The city probably represented the sort of tolerance that Laurens sought. There at least he was out of danger from the horrors of the Inquisition.

On arrival, he rested himself on the steps of a fairly opulent house, which turned out to be the home of a silk manufacturer of some importance, who came out to enquire what he was about, and who he was.

In the course of their conversation it emerged that the man himself had also once sought refuge in Frankfurt, closely paralleling Laurens' experience. The man's name is not definitely known but it could have been Van Nynove, for, as will be seen, this was the name of his niece.

He obviously felt sorry for Laurens and liked him, as he took him in, and offered him work. Noticing that Laurens' hands were not accustomed to manual labour, he gave him the job of managing his books and accounts, and managing the labour force. The condition of Laurens' hands probably showed him too that he did not come from humble stock.

At this early stage, then, Laurens' fortunes had started to change. He had a reasonably senior job and somewhere to eat and sleep, and he had avoided the Inquisition. He had formed as well an important friendship with the elderly man, now his employer.

Laurens in fact had become a Huguenot refugee from Catholic persecution. Like other Huguenots the work ethic was to be very important to him. It went hand in hand with his religion, and there seems little doubt that Laurens worked hard for his new employer, and benefitted, in turn, by acquiring knowledge of the silk trade, which was to stand him, and those that came after him, in such good stead later on.

Exactly how long Laurens stayed in Frankfurt is unclear, but certainly long enough for him to be treated as one of the family, as is powerfully underlined by the fact that he married the silk manufacturer's niece, one Barbara Nynove. The match was to be a lasting and happy one, producing seven children, and only to end many years later with Barbara's death in England.

Some time later Barbara's uncle died. When this took place is not known, but it is known that the whole of his wealth passed to Barbara, who was the sole heir to his fortune. This death, together with their new-found wealth, had a profound influence on their lives.

Unfortunately the history of Laurens and Barbara becomes obscure at this point through dearth of documentation. It is known that they decided to leave Frankfurt and come to England. It is known too that they crossed the Channel to Sandwich and settled there. What is not known are the reasons for their move. Speculation must replace fact in the hope that the gap between the two is not too great.

It is quite possible that they did not trust Frankfurt to remain forever the safe haven it had been, since the Duke of Alva, under orders from his king, was spreading his persecutions over an ever larger area. It was a period of turmoil, and Laurens probably felt that he and Barbara were, once more, in danger from the same sources of repression that had beset him before. Perhaps too they saw commercial opportunities in England from which they might take advantage with reasonable safety, as Elizabeth I had replaced Mary, her Catholic sister, on the throne of England. Perhaps they had word that some of their friends had already crossed the Channel, and they wished to join them. Whatever the reason, they did cross the Channel, and they lived for a while in Sandwich.

In Sandwich, there is a church of some charm that was used by the Huguenots. It is of the type that has a gallery running around three sides of the building, and the pillars that support those galleries are the masts of some of the ships that carried Huguenot migrants from France to Kent. It is probable, though, that the church was not built by the time that Laurens arrived, but was used by subsequent waves of refugees. If the church did exist then, they would have used it, almost certainly, as their place of worship.

Laurens and Barbara stayed in Sandwich until 1575. By that time Laurens was 39 years old. In that year, for some reason or other, the Privy Council of England decided to move a number of the 'better off' émigrés from Sandwich to Canterbury. The decision was implemented by the Lord Warden of the Cinque Ports, and, as Laurens and Barbara were amongst those 'better off', to Canterbury they moved.

The move probably suited them very well. In Canterbury Laurens was able to deploy his silk-making skills to his advantage. The only constraint that the authorities placed upon the migrants was that they should not compete for trade with the local people. This, in effect, meant that they were to manufacture only light cloths such as silks, bayes and grossegraines, in that way allowing the resident English weavers to continue weaving the heavier cloths, as had always been their practice.

The system worked well, and the foreigners were in no way resented by the English. On the contrary, they were made welcome by the local residents, and were popular.

At this time Laurens started to play an active part in church affairs. In 1577 he was made a deacon of the Walloon Church in Canterbury, and shortly after that he was made an Elder. In the Cathedral, services in French were held in the Black Prince's Chapel every Sunday. Similar services have been held in the same Chapel of Canterbury Cathedral each week since 1547. Such services are conducted by a French Pasteur of the Protestant faith, and attract a congregation to this day. In those days, long ago, it must have been a signal to the Huguenots that they were acceptable.

It is known that Laurens attended a 'Colloque'[2] in Southampton, a city where many Huguenots established their homes, and only a few miles from where Longford Castle was to be completed in 1592 by Sir Thomas and Lady Gorges, and in which Laurens' descendants were to live following its purchase in 1717 by Sir Edward Des Bouverie from Lord Coleraine, the then owner.

In 1591 Laurens' wife Barbara died. She had borne Laurens seven children, and, by all accounts, she and Laurens had been happy together. What is certain is that their life together had passed through many changes, taking them from their French origins towards a truly English life.

This is perhaps best described by the family motto 'Patria Cara Carior Libertas' (My country is dear, but Liberty is dearer). Dear France had already been exchanged for the freedom of England.

[2] A type of Seminar

Laurens married again in 1594 one Catherine Pipelart, and in 1604 they moved to Threadneedle Street in the City of London. This possibly signified a massive step forward in Laurens' attitude to business, as opportunities to accrue wealth were there to be exploited.

So far as religion was concerned, Laurens was able to keep up his connection with the church in Canterbury, whilst at the same time establishing himself within the church in Threadneedle Street.

He died a moderately rich man in 1610 at the age of seventy-four.

He was survived by all seven of his children. They were all Barbara's. His second wife Catherine Pipelart bore him none.

Samuel, Laurens' eldest son, married Elizabeth Forterie. He was in the silk trade. He died sometime before 1621 and she in 1625. His second son, Jacob, was born in Canterbury and educated at Leiden University. He married three times and had four children of whom Daniel, son of Marie Gaillet, became the Des Bouveries' agent in Amsterdam. This, though, was not to be the main family line of descent.

It fell to his third son, Edward, to provide this link. Edward married Mary Formestraux at the church in Threadneedle Street; she, in turn, produced four children. The rest of Laurens' family consisted of John, who died before 1610, and Elizabeth, who was born in Canterbury in 1593, and produced nine children, one of whom, Jeanne, married into the Du Cane family. Jeanne was born in Canterbury and married a Norwich silk merchant. Norwich, like Southampton, had become a Huguenot centre. Finally, Lea married a Forterie, who, like Laurens, came from Lille.

They were Huguenots, and they all married Huguenots, which was encouraged by the English. They settled down to business and English life without much trouble. This was probably because French Huguenots had something very positive to add to English life. They brought with them their skills in banking, medicine, silver-making, the military, arts and much else, not least, perhaps, a fondness for growing decorative plants in competition with each other. This brought to England the concept of the 'Flower Show', which was to become so popular over the years, and still survives today.

Some believe that Marlborough would never have won his wars without his French Huguenot Generals, the most distinguished of whom was Ligonier, who first commanded the Grenadier Guards, and finally the British Army itself.

Laurens was one of this band. He brought with him knowledge of fine silk manufacture and a strong duty towards his religion. He also brought with him a great dislike of persecution, which could have been in part why his successors were to hold radical and liberal political views as subsequent generations engaged in politics.

It has to be said too that his successors were to prove to be bold, imaginative and hardworking.

*Signature of Laurens Des Bouverie*

*Edward Des Bouverie*
(Follower of Mierveldt)

# CHAPTER II

# *Edward Des Bouverie 1588-1625*

Not a great deal is known about Laurens' son Edward. He married a Mary Formestraux and between them they produced three daughters and a son, Sir Edward Des Bouverie, subject of the next chapter.

Edward was described as a 'merchant', and no doubt he played an important part in the development of the family business. The business itself was the promotion of trade through the Middle East with the Far East. The vehicle for this trade was the Turkey Company, operating under a charter granted by Queen Elizabeth I. Edward had two brothers older than himself. The older, Samuel, married Elizabeth Forterie, who produced a family of three. It seems, though, that at this point the family virtually ceased to exist because of the ravages of the plague. Jacob, next in age, married Elizabeth Formestraux firstly, and secondly, Marie Gaillet. The latter produced a son, Daniel, who was to become the family's agent in Amsterdam.

It is fairly apparent that large gaps in the family at this point owe much to the plague, resulting in the burial of a number of Des Bouveries in the churches in Threadneedle Street and St Benet Fink.

Sometime during this period the Levant Company was unable to hold a directors' meeting, as nearly all of the directors had died from the plague.

Edward's business was, in fact, based in Threadneedle Street. Convoys of ships were dispatched to Constantinople, where goods were trans-shipped, and carried to Aleppo, and then by way of Basra to India, Burma and the Far East by camel train.

This was a two-way traffic. From England were exported lead, tin, made-up silks, rabbit skins and much else. The reverse trade probably consisted of spices, wines, raw silk, angora, mohair and other goods that were unobtainable in England. It was a profitable trade. Sir Roy Strong in his *The Story of Britain* notes that 'the wealth of its merchants and of the trading companies such as the East India, the Royal African and the Levant company, was prodigious'. It should be noted, too, that so were the risks and dangers.

The traders themselves often lived far from home, and sometimes died far from home. There are Des Bouverie graves in Aleppo, Constantinople and Cyprus. They were exposed to strange diseases, and were the prey of pirates, or endangered by storms at sea. Those, though, who survived became rich. To emphasise one of the dangers, it was quite common in family wills to leave money to redeem friends captured by Barbary pirates, and subsequently held to ransom.

*Excerpt from Daniel Des Bouverie's commonplace book written in Flemish*

Edward died in 1625 and lies buried at St Benet Fink.

In spite of the fact that there is little recorded about this Edward, nevertheless he must be considered important, as it seems that under his guidance the family export-import business really began to take shape. His older brothers might have done as well, but it would appear their families were either cut down by the plague, or followed some other interest.

22

*Sir Edward Des Bouverie*
(Friedrich Kerseboom)

# CHAPTER III

## *Sir Edward Des Bouverie 1621-1694*

It seems that this Edward, son of the subject of the previous chapter, was the first member of the family to move from the coffee shops in the City to the Levant itself. Indicative of his wealth is the fact that James I knighted him on board one of his own ships. He owned a considerable fleet.

He married Anne Forterie in Threadneedle Street. She produced for him a large and important family.

How long Edward spent abroad is a matter for conjecture. He and Anne had eleven children, and it is very doubtful if wives went with their husbands to the Levant. Most of the traders based there tended to be bachelors. Possibly then it is wrong to assume that he was a physical presence for very long in Aleppo or Constantinople. His sons Jacob, Peter, John and Christopher certainly all resided in either of those two towns. It is quite possible, then, that their father, Edward, was based in Threadneedle Street, just going with one of his convoys to Constantinople, and then on to Aleppo, only to return to the City of London.

It was during this period that the Des Bouveries made money. They probably made a great deal of money. At the same time, they held positions of importance and responsibility.

William, the eldest son, who was to carry the Des Bouverie line forward into the next generation, was appointed Governor of the Bank of England in 1707. He was knighted in 1713, and created a baronet in the following year. He first married Mary Edwards, and, secondly, Anne Urry.

Edward's son, Jacob, was a merchant agent in Aleppo. His other distinction was that he bought 'The Honour and Lordship' of Folkestone and Terlingham from Sir Basil Dixwell. The next in age, Peter, was a merchant agent in Constantinople.

*An account taken from the books of Jacob Des Bouverie (1659-1722)*

He worked there, died there, and is buried there. John was in Aleppo as a merchant, where he probably worked with his brother Jacob. He died at sea, and is buried in Cyprus.

Finally, Christopher, who was knighted as Sir William was in 1713, worked in Aleppo as his brothers did. He married one Elizabeth Freeman of Betchworth in Surrey. He distinguished himself by being one of the first directors of the South Sea Company. He made the wise decision, though, to sell his shares just before that company foundered. He was not, then, affected by the bursting of the 'Bubble'.

Other sons were Edward, who was born at Caen, and Daniel, who died young. Neither they nor the four daughters, Jane, Anne, Mary and Elizabeth have a role in this narrative.

The family presence in the Levant was not destined to persist. Land ownership in Folkestone, though, is still a part of the family business.

*Anne Forterie, wife of Sir Edward Des Bouverie*
(Friedrich Kerseboom)

25

Edward died in 1694. His death is said to have been hurried on by the fact that one of his convoys was caught in a terrible storm off Gibraltar. Three of his sons, possibly Peter, John and Sir Christopher, were sailing with the convoy. They all survived the storm, but the damage to the fleet amounted to £20,000, a huge sum in those days. Ships must have foundered, but the tale gives an idea of the size to which the business had grown. It was both large and successful, and was to continue.

The shock of the great storm affected Edward's health, and he died soon after in 1694.

*Account relating to John Des Bouverie.*
*One entry relates to a cargo salvaged from a burnt Dutch ship.*

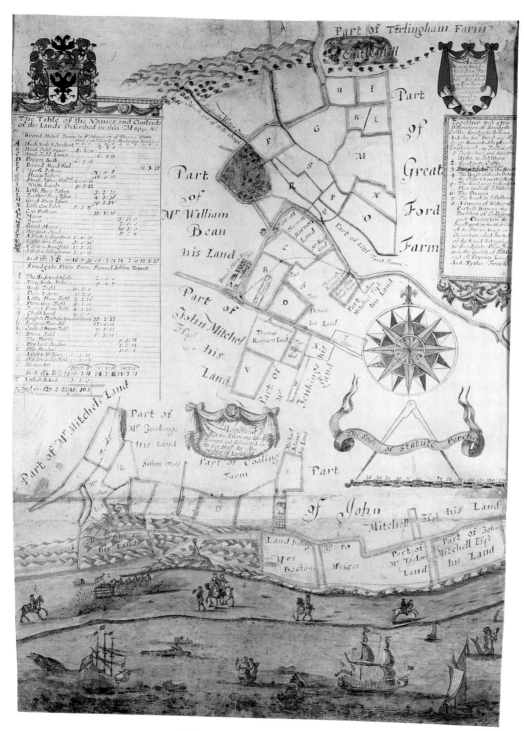

*Old map of Folkestone, 1698*

27

28

*Sir William Des Bouverie*
(Sir Godfrey Kneller)

# CHAPTER IV

# *Sir William Des Bouverie 1656-1717*

William was the eldest of Sir Edward's large family. During his reign business with and within the Levant must have reached a peak, and nearly all William's brothers played an active part. If they had not, it might well have been difficult to maintain trade within that area on the scale that was, in fact, accomplished.

William himself enjoyed a distinguished life. His first wife, Mary Edwards, bore him only one child, who died in infancy, and Mary herself died soon after. His second wife, Anne Urry, produced six children who survived and six that died in infancy. The picture of Mary and her child painted by Friedrich Kerseboom is a little sad. Neither can have lived long after its completion.

There were three important milestones in William's business life. In 1707 he was appointed Governor of the Bank of England. In 1713 he was knighted by Queen Anne and in 1714 he was created a baronet. For what particular service to the nation or the monarch these honours were bestowed upon him is not recorded. It can be safely accepted, though, that he was an important and distinguished man so far as the business of the nation was concerned.

His four active brothers were Jacob, Peter, John and Christopher.

Jacob was the family's agent in Aleppo. In spite of this, and in spite of the distance involved between the Levant and England, he purchased the Honour and Lordship of Folkestone and Terlingham from Sir Basil Dixwell. The town evidently was in a run down state, but in spite of modern laws relating to leasehold enfranchisement, significant areas still remain in family ownership. Dixwell Road in the west end of Folkestone is so named today.

William's other brothers have already been described, and little is known of

*Mary Edwards, 1st wife of Sir William Des Bouverie with her son Edward*
(Friedrich Kerseboom)

*Anne Urry, 2nd wife of Sir William Des Bouverie*
(Sir Godfrey Kneller)

31

William's sisters except that Mary and Elizabeth died young, whilst Jane and Anne were married to John d'Eau and Sir Philip Boteler of Kent respectively.

It should be mentioned that despite very considerable activity during this period, signs were beginning to appear that trade with the Levant Company, and within the area it operated, was deteriorating, and that huge profits, or indeed any profits at all, might soon be a thing of the past.

The construction of ships had improved so that they were able to sail round the Cape of Good Hope to the Far East, in this way disposing of the need for an overland journey by camel train. At the same time, trade with America was increasing rapidly, and was providing strong competition. By the same token, the East India Company, a powerful corporate body, was found to be in even more direct competition with the Turkey and Levant companies. Finally the area in which the traders lived and operated, namely Turkey, was entering a period of political instability, and was at war with Persia. First then there was direct competition and secondly the mechanics of trade were disrupted. Change was in the air.

The family had obviously been doing well and living in far away places may not have been as great a hardship as might be imagined for an émigré family. Even so, a gradual disinvestment from the Levant business was thought to be a sensible strategy to follow. As the trade that they had been used to faded, the alternative investment chosen was the purchase of land in England. The change was a gradual one. The last Des Bouverie actually to live for a while in Turkey was Edward Des Bouverie, William's eldest son, who purchased Longford in 1717 from Lord Coleraine.

It is interesting to note that no attempt was made to construct a fleet of larger vessels that would be capable of continuing the trade with the East. The risks perhaps were too great.

Sir William and his brothers then were active merchants plying between England and the Levant, or living more or less permanently in the latter. His children too were active in the same way, but after that generation there were to be no more Des Bouveries in Aleppo, Constantinople or Cyprus.

It would be wrong for the reader to feel that life in these far away places was unpleasant. Admittedly there were the dangers already outlined, but the traders from France, Italy and England lived in an enjoyable society, isolated from the local population in Khans or compounds.

Danger was more evident in the journey to and from the Levant. If accomplished by sea there were the hazards of storms and the very real danger of capture by the Barbary pirates. Because of these dangers, quite frequently an overland journey was undertaken. The route chosen would be to Venice and then by way of Belgrade and Sofia to Constantinople.

William and his brothers, then, represent the family's most active period of trade with the Far East through Turkey. The trade was both interesting and lucrative, and during their time it possibly reached its zenith, but it was to decline and fade away in the not too distant future.

William himself died in 1717 – the year his son purchased Longford Castle in Wiltshire.

34

*Sir Edward Des Bouverie*
(Michael Dahl)

# CHAPTER V

# Sir Edward Des Bouverie, Bt 1688-1736

Sir Edward, eldest son of Sir William, carried on the family business. He married Mary Smith in 1718. They had no children and he never married again. Mary Smith herself died in 1721. She was the first Bouverie to be buried at St Peter's, Britford in which parish lies Longford Castle.

The previous generation had made money in all probability such as they could never have imagined. It was becoming steadily more apparent, though, that trade through the Levant was deteriorating to such an extent that it would be wise to change the emphasis of family business with a certain degree of urgency.

As already indicated, this was accomplished by buying land in England, which, at the time, was considered a good investment. Jacob (1659-1722) had already purchased Folkestone, which, although run down, produced a decent income (including, amongst other things, a toll on all the crabs that were landed in the harbour). Edward wished to consolidate his landholding round Southampton, but, in the event, land was bought and sold all over the place.

The land purchase that was to affect the family in the happiest of ways was the purchase of Longford Castle from Lord Coleraine in 1717.

The land had originally been owned by the Cervingtons. For some reason or other they had become impoverished, and the land passed into the hands of Sir Thomas and Lady Gorges. Lady Gorges was Queen Elizabeth's chief Lady-in-Waiting and a native of Sweden. Sir Thomas was Gentleman Usher of the Privy Chamber, and Governor of Hurst Castle on the Isle of Wight. They decided to build a triangular, Swedish pattern castle on the banks of the River Avon, the three towers representing Father, Son and Holy Ghost. The subsoil, though, was treacherous, and the whole house-building operation became very expensive.

There was not the money to finish the job.

At this time the Spanish Armada was defeated in the Western Channel, and blown up the Channel by a westerly gale.

Sir Thomas, well-placed at Hurst Castle, knew of one wreck that had great wealth in it, which apparently consisted of gold and silver bars and iron shot. With, one imagines, little difficulty, he persuaded Helena, his wife, to beg it of the Queen. The Queen, in a euphoric state after winning the great battle, was giving away useless wrecks left, right and centre. The gift was made and the wealth therein provided enough money to complete the construction of Longford.

It is said that Sir Edward saw this castle in the valley as he rode by on his way to the West Country. He fell in love with it, and purchased it from the Coleraines there and then. He is said to have had enough money in his saddle bags to effect the purchase. The purchase was made just 149 years after Laurens's flight from home.

Edward, quite apart from the purchase of Longford, had an interesting history. His training as a merchant started in 1700, when he was twelve years old. At this tender age he was dispatched to Aleppo to be apprenticed to his uncle Sir Christopher Des Bouverie (1671-1722).

His journey to the Levant must have been a testing one. He would have been accompanied on his journey, which may have taken him overland to Venice, and then on by sea to his destination. Alternatively, as previously outlined, he may have taken the route by land all the way via Belgrade and Sofia.

The point of travelling by land was to avoid capture by the pirates, who rampaged across the Mediterranean. A number of Bouverie wills at this time leave money for the redemption of friends who might be held to ransom by those marauders.

Whether by land or sea it would be a hard journey for a twelve-year-old.

It is not clear where he worked in the Levant. Sir Christopher to whom he was apprenticed had houses in Constantinople, Aleppo and Cyprus. It is known though that he ended up running his own cloth business in Cyprus and keeping accounts and records personal to himself.

*Mary Smith, later the wife of Sir Edward Des Bouverie*
(Friedrich Kerseboom)

*Family account relating to sale of silk from Burma*

By 1710 Sir Edward became ever more aware that his business was deteriorating. The recession that the family was experiencing is perhaps best summed up in a letter from Jacob, Edward's brother, who was travelling in the Low Countries. He wrote 'Can get no money, because merchants being almost entirely broke, or else not having any confidence at all in ours in England.'

Sir Christopher, his uncle, to whom he had been apprenticed in Aleppo, had already returned to England to join in partnership with one Nathaniel Harley. The trade at which they worked was probably of a general nature.

In 1712, Edward himself returned to England. He was to be the last of the Des Bouveries to live and work at the eastern end of the Mediterranean. There was never to be a Des Bouverie presence there again, although the business continued for a while, albeit somewhat muted.

It is on record at Longford that this, his final journey from the Levant, was made easier and safer by the grant of a licence from Queen Anne, which was countersigned by the French authorities, allowing him to cross France.

Mary Smith whom he married in 1718 left no children; she died three years later. Edward never married again, and since his next brother in age William had already died in Constantinople (1709), his heir became his brother Jacob.

Edward died in 1736, rather surprisingly in Aix-la-Chapelle. Perhaps the wily old trader was off on his travels again.

# CHAPTER VI

# *Sir Jacob Des Bouverie*
# *1st Viscount Folkestone 1694-1761*

Jacob inherited from his brother Edward. He was a member of the Middle Temple from the age of fourteen, and continued his education thereafter at Christchurch, Oxford, and by means of a European tour.

He was to be a notable member of the family, and it was he who decided that after all the years that England had been the family home and provider of safety, friendship and wealth, it was time to become English. The matter was accomplished by Act of Parliament in 1736. The family name was changed from Des Bouverie to Bouverie, and the migrant family had settled down.

In 1747 he was created both Baron Longford and Viscount Folkestone. He was now not only a man of very considerable property, but also ennobled.

He worked at his properties. Folkestone, in particular, was in a very run-down state, and he spent much time, thought and money beautifying Longford both within and without.

It is not the task of this narrative to detail the wonders he created at Longford. They are recorded well in account books and various catalogues. It is true, though, that he and his son William after him, exercising great good taste, made Longford – the house, its interior, and the park – into a very beautiful place complementing its own superb situation. Both father and son had imagination, which coincided happily with a period replete with good craftsmen, designers and painters. Much of the result of their far-reaching imagination and enthusiasm can still be enjoyed today.

Jacob's grandson was also to play his part in this process, but his efforts remain for another chapter. Jacob worked to a fairly robust scale. He designed, or had designed, the park, planting many trees. He designed a garden, a kitchen garden

*Sir Jacob Des Bouverie, later 1st Viscount Folkestone, as a young man*
(Michael Dahl)

*Mary Clarke, 1st wife of Sir Jacob Des Bouverie*
(Jean-Baptiste Van Loo)

*Elizabeth Marsham, 2nd wife of Sir Jacob Des Bouverie, later 1st Viscount Folkestone*
(Jean-Baptiste Van Loo)

and stables. He flattened only recently formed watermeadows, and worked away at much else. Some of his trees probably stand today, notably the huge planes and the chestnut grove. Others only recently fell, the victims of two hurricanes (1987 and 1991).

Jacob married firstly Mary Clarke and, secondly, Elizabeth Marsham. Mary died in 1739, and is buried at Britford. She had seven children. Her eldest son, William, was to become the first Earl of Radnor.

*The Act of Parliament changing the name of various Des Bouveries to 'Bouverie'*

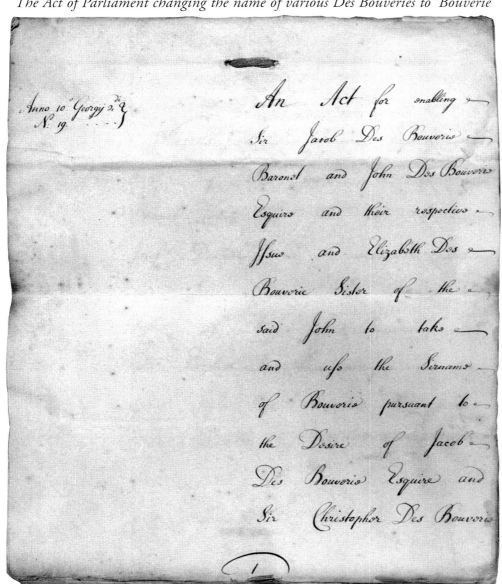

43

Jacob's ties with Salisbury, notwithstanding his very substantial ownership in Folkestone, were very strong. He was made a Freeman of the city, and, in 1741, Salisbury sent him to Parliament as their member. Three years later he was appointed Recorder to the city, and, at the same time, was made Deputy Lieutenant of Wiltshire.

He was one of the main promoters of the Society of Arts, Manufactures and Commerce, which was brought into being by William Shipley. He was elected the Society's first president, with his brother-in-law, Lord Romney, holding the post of vice-president. Jacob fulfilled this particular duty until his death.

William, seventh Earl of Radnor, was to fill the same position as his ancestor in the Society's double centennial year. Jacob was painted and hangs in the Society's rooms in John Adam Street. The painting was accomplished by Gainsborough after Jacob's death. He copied a Hudson portrait and added legs from his imagination. William, seventh Earl, was also painted, and his picture hangs there as well, but in an obscure part of the building. The artist was Rodrigo Moynihan. The artist was hesitant and slow. The sitter was bored. The picture was a disaster.

For Jacob, it seems that life at Longford was good. Not himself a hunter, he employed a gamekeeper from Charlton-all-Saints to keep him supplied with game. His name was Reeves, and he was also a shoemaker by trade. He kept Longford well supplied. Most popular of all was venison from the New Forest.

Almost certainly, though, Jacob was a fisherman. He kept a boat and fishing tackle. Records show that salmon were caught, the largest being one of $21\frac{1}{2}$ lbs (1746).

He raced at Stockbridge until racing ceased there, and afterwards at Salisbury where a course had been built as a replacement. He supported the Salisbury music festival, he was a good Member of Parliament and a good Recorder. When he returned to Longford after spells away, church bells were rung in Salisbury and Britford (a practice now discontinued).

It seems he lived life to the full and his popularity cannot be in doubt.

*Jacob, 1st Viscount Folkestone, after ennoblement*
(Thomas Hudson)

*William, 1st Earl of Radnor*
(Thomas Gainsborough)

# CHAPTER VII

# William Bouverie, 2nd Viscount Folkestone, 1st Earl of Radnor 1724-1776

William's mother was Mary Clarke. Her father was Bartholomew Clarke, himself a Turkey merchant. William continued the family connection with the Levant through governorship of the Levant Company. He succeeded the Earl of Shaftesbury in this position in 1771. The Earl of Shaftesbury was married to Mary, William's sister. William was re-elected to this position annually until his death. Like his father, though, his leanings were towards land and politics.

At home at Longford he set about the beautifying of Longford with even more vigour than his father.

William married three times. In order his wives were: Harriot Pleydell, daughter of, and heiress to, Sir Mark Pleydell of Coleshill; Rebecca Alleyne, daughter of John Alleyne of Four Hills, Barbados; and finally, Anne Hales, Dowager Countess of Feversham.

Harriot was by all accounts a person of great charm. Sadly she was destined to die young, shortly after giving birth to a son and heir, who was to become the second Earl of Radnor. Sadly too, her father, Sir Mark Pleydell, did not get on well with William. Dislike is probably too strong a word to use, but it would be an understatement to say they were not great friends.

Nevertheless, Harriot was to have inherited the Pleydell fortune and lands, and her father added a codicil to his will leaving everything to her son Jacob. Already on William's marriage to Harriot the name Pleydell had been attached by hyphen to that of Bouverie. So came into the family another name of eight letters, a beautiful house designed by Roger Pratt (burnt down in 1952), and considerable lands and wealth.

*Harriot Pleydell, 1st wife of William, 1st Earl of Radnor*
(Thomas Hudson)

*Rebecca Alleyne, 2nd wife of William, 1st Earl of Radnor*
(Sir Joshua Reynolds)

49

50

*Anne Hales, 3rd wife of William, 1st Earl of Radnor*
(Francis Cotes)

William's second wife, Rebecca Alleyne, was the daughter of a Barbadian sugar planter of wealth and position. They produced three sons who all survived, as well as a number of other children who did not share their good fortune. Rebecca herself died in 1764, a year before her husband was created an Earl. Never destined to be Countess of Radnor, she lies buried at Britford. Her picture by Sir Joshua Reynolds depicts a very beautiful woman with just a hint that her blood may not be entirely Saxon.

Finally, William married Anne Hales, Dowager Countess of Feversham, who gave birth to two daughters. Sadly both of them died in infancy and she produced no more.

A detailed study of the full family tree, held at Longford, brings into perspective the appalling rate of infant deaths in the eighteenth century. The imagination can fill in the periods of sorrow and distress that this must have caused.

Rebecca's three boys and Jacob, Harriot's child, were all given the best education possible. For the most part, they went to Harrow and Oxford, and did well, but in all probability they benefitted greatly from their father's choice of tutor, one Dr Samuel Glasse. Dr Glasse was a native of Wiltshire and a notable theologian. William himself was greatly impressed by this man and contributed money towards two of his societies, both of which had a strong religious orientation. Glasse repaid the compliment by proposing that William become a member of the Royal Society, Glasse himself being already a member of that august body.

Although the boys were put through a rigorous academic upbringing, it is quite clear that at Longford there was much to enjoy. Archery and shooting, fishing and all manner of games saw to it that all work and no play was not, in fact, the order of the day.

William's popularity was such that when, after marriage to Anne in Hanover Square, they returned to Longford on July 31st, the ringers of six churches in Salisbury rang out their peels, as did the ringers in Alderbury.[1] In addition in the churches there were for the occasion, 'drummers to drum and musicians to play'. Who organised all this cacophony of sound history does not relate.

[1] A village adjacent to Longford

In 1761 William moved from the Commons to the Lords on the death of his father. He had been MP for Salisbury since 1747. In 1765 he was created an Earl, picking up the Earldom of Radnor previously held by the Robartes family until their male line ran out. In 1768 he was granted leave to use the double-headed Eagle as his coat of arms, with the very pertinent motto 'Patria Cara Carior Libertas'. At Longford there is a somewhat enigmatic document, which takes the form of a petition to the King, George the Second. The petitioner appears to be the second Earl, and he asks if he might have a simple escutcheon leaving out his mother's quarterings, as there were too many of them. It appears that this request was made whilst he was still Viscount Folkestone. At the end of the petition, firmly scrawled, by his father are the words: 'I disapprove of this  R.'

The banner, though, that flies over Longford to this day is of a double-headed Eagle with a simple shield on which is a device exactly the same as one crudely drawn on the back of the picture of Laurens, depicted at the beginning of this tale.

In many other ways he was vigorous. In the line of business he acquired properties dotted about between Durham and Cornwall. This, without doubt, is a vague description, but the fact is that he went all over England for his acquisitions. The original idea that he formed was to consolidate all his properties within Dorset and Wiltshire and around Southampton. This concept, in the event, was obviously a failure.

The Folkestone properties once more needed special attention, not this time because of poverty and neglect, but because of the threat of invasion from France.

Folkestone, as it is to this day, was important. The revenues that came therefrom were substantial and from many quarters.

At home, William, Earl of Radnor, continued apace the improvements to Longford that had already been started by Edward and Jacob. He bought many pictures, seventy-nine in all. He bought and had made splendid furniture. At the same time, he continued landscaping the park and planting trees.

He built a chapel, which the next generation destroyed, and he built a mausoleum against the north side of Britford church to accommodate those yet to die, including himself. He purchased Rysbrack's statue of Fame and placed it in a prominent position in the park towards Salisbury. The statue is of an angel holding a shield on which is sculpted the features of King Arthur, who was considered a suitable candidate for this honour. To the relief of everyone Rysbrack's first choice, the Duke of Cumberland, victor of Culloden, was discarded.

Poverty and sickness in England at this time were an ongoing problem brought to the fore locally by a riot of poor people in the market square in Salisbury over the price of wheat. So serious was it that the army had to be called in to deal with the situation.

William, himself, was generous to the poor, and, when on his death Lord Feversham left £3,500 for the poor, a committee was formed to bring into being the Salisbury Infirmary. A site was chosen. A building was built, and William, Earl of Radnor, was elected President.

Amongst other local duties and initiatives, William gave support to the first proper local newspaper, the *Salisbury and Winchester Journal*, which was started by the Collins family. He involved himself, too, in the repair of the Salisbury Town House. He seemed to have a finger in every pie. Not least he raced, enjoyed a good ball, and gave the Mayor and Corporation a sumptuous lunch once a year.

He died in 1776, the year of America's Independence, and his obituary related 'An active and benevolent member of society, an affectionate and judicious parent, and a loyal and independent Peer of the Realm.'

Perhaps the adjective 'independent' accounts for much of the behaviour of the title holder or head of the family both before and after the first Earl's death.

# CHAPTER VIII

# Jacob, 2nd Earl of Radnor 1749-1828

Jacob inherited the title in 1776 at the start of the American War of Independence. He married in 1777 Anne Duncombe, step-daughter of Anne Hales, Dowager Countess of Feversham, being the 3rd wife of his father. They produced a family of five sons: William, Duncombe, Laurence, Frederick and Philip, and three daughters, all of whom died relatively young.

Jacob's time as Earl of Radnor was a turbulent one in so far as the world at large was concerned. During that period there took place the French Revolution; followed by the Napoleonic wars; the War of Independence with America as well as the war of 1812 with the same country; and, at that time too, a little known war with the Argentine Republic (1807).

Of his children, William was to inherit; Duncombe was to have a distinguished naval career; Laurence was called to the Bar, but died of consumption at an early age; Frederick was Rector first of Hambledon, Surrey, and secondly of Pewsey: he was notable for having six boys and seven girls. The members of this substantial family all survived. Philip was a banker and looked after his father's finances, and after him came three daughters all of whom died young.

On assuming the title, like his two predecessors, Jacob became Recorder of Salisbury. No longer able to represent Salisbury as that city's representative in the House of Commons, he was able to pursue politics in the Lords.

Politically he was a Whig. Not only was he a Whig, but he was a Whig of radical inclinations. He is described as 'sticking up for the rights of the people'. He wrote to George Washington just before that gentleman's death telling him, in so many words, that by no means everyone felt he had behaved improperly in fighting for, and winning, the freedom of America from England. He received a long and courteous reply.

The Speech of
The Earl of Radnor in the House
of Lords March 5th: 1778 on the second
Reading of the Bill intituled an
Act to enable his Majesty to
appoint Commissioners with suf
ficient Powers to treat consult and
agree upon the Means of quieting
the Disorders now subsisting in
certain of the Colonies Plantations
and Provinces in North America

a My Lords I wish (If I may
meet with so much Indulgence) to
draw your Lordships Attention to

*Preamble to a speech in the House of Lords of the second Earl.
The subject is the American War of Independence.*

55

56

*Jacob, Viscount Folkestone, later 2nd Earl of Radnor*
(Nathaniel Dance)

*The Hon Anne Duncombe, wife of Jacob, 2nd Earl of Radnor*
(Sir Joshua Reynolds)

He travelled in France frequently, taking Anne with him, and, on other occasions, his eldest son William. They stayed both in Paris and Caen. In the latter town they rented a house, and were well known and much liked by the townspeople.

On one trip to Paris they were introduced to Marie Antoinette and Louis XVI. On another journey Jacob and his son William were conducted round the Bastille on the day after it was stormed.

Illustrated here is a piece of paper which when folded, reads 'Vive la reine le dauphin et le roy'. Unfolded it reveals a bar or two of the 'Marseillaise' and the inscription 'Vive la nation la liberté et la loix'. Whether it was of practical use on this trip, or just an amusing exercise in cartography can only be guessed at.

Not long after this particular sortie to France Jacob joined the Militia, first as an Ensign from which junior position he was soon promoted to Captain. It is probable, though, that his real contribution to the defence of the realm was monetary and organisational.

In Wiltshire he helped organise the Militia. In Kent he subscribed money to help form the East Kent Militia and, since his grandmother had inherited Delapré Abbey in Northamptonshire, he became involved there as well.

During all these military involvements the Prince of Wales[1] decided to descend on Stockbridge for the races. His visit turned out to be a major event.

His Royal Highness, as well as attending the races, attended a ball held in his honour in the Assembly Rooms in Salisbury. Before the ball, he dined at Longford. The event is recorded in the form of a table plan showing how the food was laid out. Sadly there is no record of who came to eat it.

The ball itself started at 11.00 p.m. and supper was served at 2 a.m. Even so, everyone was ready for the races again the next day.

Inserted into the proceedings was a visit by His Royal Highness to the Episcopal palace. Lord Radnor introduced him to all the Councillors and then apparently delivered a notable address.

Perhaps more important was the fact that, to the despair of future generations, Jacob employed James Wyatt to change Longford from a reasonably modest chateau into a hexagonal palace. It was a fateful decision that boded ill both for the present and the future.

Wyatt worked away. He destroyed one of the Elizabethan towers and replaced it with a larger one of his own design. He then built two more to the east and south east, each joined to the other by substantial edifices.

It seemed that Jacob then had a difference of opinion with him, since Wyatt then moved off to build Fonthill[2]. He was replaced as architect by Daniel Alexander, but the concept of creating a palace was never accomplished, and it was left to the fourth Earl to put Humpty-Dumpty together again.

[1] Later George IV
[2] For William Beckford

In 1785 the Mayor and Corporation of Salisbury held a dinner in the Town House. By all accounts it was a very good dinner, which may or may not lead one to believe that it had something to do with the Town House catching fire when the diners had gone home. It was severely damaged.

Attempts were made to repair it, but they were ineffective. At that point the Earl of Radnor stepped in, donated land for a Guildhall, and, with his own architect, built the Guildhall that stands today.

There was something of a wrangle after this apparent act of great generosity. Jacob wished to receive a toll on produce sold in the market to help defray some of his costs. The corporation thought differently. An argument ensued. The corporation won.

William, the eldest son, will be the subject of the next chapter. Here, though, a glance, or even more than glance should be directed towards the younger children.

Duncombe, next in order of age, joined the Navy and became an Admiral of the Blue, retiring eventually as an Admiral of the Red which signified he was a very high Admiral indeed. He retired to become a Member of Parliament. His career in the Navy was a long one, and his voyages took him all over the world. Throughout his career he kept a diary, and he wrote to his father on a regular basis so far as his duties allowed.

Contemplating retirement, at the end of his naval career, he was seriously worried that his naval career might have moulded him too coarse for not only Parliament but even more so for the drawing-room and the company of women.

In one letter to his father, starting as always, 'My Lord', he comments that there is just time to write before returning to Santander to bombard the town 'for the second time today', adding, 'His Grace[1] will be well pleased with us for blowing up the bridges behind Soult's[2] retreat'. He writes too from Buenos Aires, where he has difficulty in preventing his crew from defecting. He acquires a seal-skin canoe in Newfoundland 'as your Lordship may find it useful on the river at home', and much else.

[1] The Duke of Wellington
[2] Napoleon's marshal

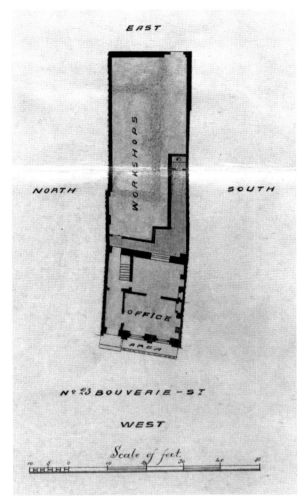

*Crude working drawing for a building in Bouverie Street*
*(probably early nineteenth century)*

A little sadly he writes from Poole asking if his father would like to come aboard his ship when it docked at Portsmouth – 'As your Lordship has never been on board any of my ships'. In the same letter he writes – 'We are here pressing crew, an unchristian but necessary duty'. The next in age was Laurence. Unwell, he accomplished little and died young.

Frederick was quite different. He was tutored by the Rev Morres whilst still at

61

*Corner of Bouverie and Pleydell Streets today (a recent family development)*

Oxford. Probably because of Morres's influence, he became a man of the cloth. He looked after various parishes at various times, one of which was Pewsey. His brother on inheriting became patron of Pewsey, and this duty has been passed on down the generations.

Perhaps the most notable thing about Frederick and his wife Elizabeth was the fact that they produced a family of six boys and seven daughters all of whom survived.

Frederick's youngest brother was Philip. He was a banker, helping his father with his finances.

All the daughters died young.

The second Earl, like his immediate predecessor, did much to embellish the Castle and the Park. The Wyatt idea was a disaster, but he was a friend of the painter Cosway, and added a large number of pictures to the collection, which was already substantial.

He purchased land in Whitefriars and Fleet Street. With the former purchase he formed Pleydell and Bouverie Streets. This year Number 4 Bouverie Street, which stands at the juncture with Pleydell Street, has been redeveloped in contemporary style and let. 16-32 Bouverie Street is also being redeveloped, and, with this redevelopment, the freehold interest of a very large site will accrue to the family in full in 150 years time. The game then continues.

The second Earl seems to have been a notable member of the family. Antiquarian, left-wing capitalist, collector, innovator, politician, friend of Royalty and friend of France.

He owned a good cellar and his friend, the Governor of Tobago, supplied him regularly with turtles, as he enjoyed the soup.

His strength failed before he died in 1828.

*William, 4th Viscount Folkestone, later 3rd Earl of Radnor (in youth)*
(Marie Louise Elizabeth Vigée-Lebrun)

# CHAPTER IX

# William, 3rd Earl of Radnor 1779-1869

By the time William inherited in 1828 he had already travelled over much of Europe in the course of his education. He was present with his mother and father a day after the Bastille was stormed, and spent much time with them in rented houses in Caen and Paris.

Accompanied, more often than not, by his tutor, l'Abbé de Trepan, he went at the age of fourteen years on a tour of Prussia. This was accomplished after studying both at Edinburgh and Brasenose, Oxford. To Edinburgh he took his own tutor, Mr Morres.

It is interesting to speculate whether l'Abbé de Trepan was or was not of the Roman Catholic faith. If he was, one can only note that the relationship between William and Trepan showed a marked improvement over that between Laurens and his father.

In Prussia William had a strange experience. The King of Prussia died and he attended the family funeral, and the king was interred. The next day a grand public funeral was held. Again William was there, and with pomp and circumstance, an empty coffin was buried. Presumably there was a disagreement over the site of the King of Prussia's interment to lead to such a strange accommodation.

On return from abroad, he became one of his father's Deputy Lieutenants and in 1805 he was commissioned as a Captain in the First Regiment of the Berkshire Cavalry. The country was at war with France. In spite of this he saw no action abroad. His role and that of the regiment were defensive.

William was to move from these early years to a highly political life. His life, too, was to be a long one. He missed attaining ninety years of age by one month.

He was physically a very short man. His favourite chair has very short legs and

*Lady Catherine Pelham-Clinton, Viscountess Folkestone*
(Sir William Beechey)

others have had their legs shortened to accommodate him. The impression is that, although he lived to a great age, he was not very strong and also that in youth he suffered from shyness. His mother did not allow him to hunt, shoot or bathe, and it was only when he was abroad with the Abbé that it seems he was really allowed to enjoy himself.

*Judith Anne St John Mildmay, 2nd wife of William, 3rd Earl*
(George Lethbridge Saunders)

He was a serious believer, and member of the Church of England. Amongst his writings are a number of prayers of his own composition.

He married firstly Catherine Pelham-Clinton who bore him two daughters: Catherine (1801-1875) and Frances Anne, who died in 1804. The older of the two daughters married General Edward Buckley whose home was Newhall, situated at the gates of Longford.

Secondly, William married Judith Anne, who was the daughter of Sir Henry Paulet St John Mildmay. She had five children. The eldest was to become Jacob, fourth Earl of Radnor. The second born was Edward, who was to have a distinguished parliamentary career as MP for Kilmarnock.

There then followed three daughters: Anne Maria, who died young; Jane Harriot, who married William Ellice; and Mary, who married Lord Penzance.

His character and political standpoint are perhaps best described by one of his daughters, Jane Ellice, who wrote, 'He had an intense love of the truth and justice, a ruling sense of duty and veneration for the laws of his country, but when they seemed harsh and unrighteous – such as the brutal punishments administered to the army for great or little offences, and the frightful cruelty of our criminal laws – he would spare no pains to aid in their alteration. He had a tenderness of heart, hated oppression and wrong doing, and did not shrink from stating his views'. He was, in fact, appointed a Justice of the Peace on October 6th 1801.

William's liberal views led him to support the abolition of slavery. By the same token, in 1832 he instructed the MPs of his two rotten boroughs, Salisbury and Downton, to vote for enfranchisement when the House divided on Russell's Reform Bill. His liberalism, though, did not go so far as to countenance the entry of women into the House of Lords. He put his views on this subject quite plainly: 'over my dead body'.

He was a friend of William Cobbett, MP, famous as a radical and for writing his *Rural Rides*. He contributed to a fund to help Cobbett into Parliament. He was said to be the only man with whom Cobbett had never quarrelled. Cobbett, in turn, expresses the opinion that William 'was the only man that wore a coronet, who understood the first principles of politics', and further that 'his speeches in the Upper House were the only ones worth listening to'.

Cobbett gave his friend trees that he had collected in America. They were planted at Longford, and some still stand today, such as the Acacias, and the Florida Swamp Cypress. Others were felled by two recent hurricanes in 1987 and 1991.

The passing of Russell's 1832 Act was a milestone in history, and was recognised as such in Salisbury. A great banquet was held in the market-place, and William Radnor was, so to speak, the hero of the hour, having instructed both his placemen in the rotten boroughs of Downton and Salisbury to vote for reform. He was toasted with the flowery, if not downright pompous, words as follows: 'To the health of a nobleman who had ever been and was trusted to continue to be the unflinching friend of the people and of liberal measures. A noble Lord whom the coronet did not ennoble, but who ennobled the coronet.' Fortunately, this was greeted with loud applause.

Inevitably, he became involved with the powerful controversy over the Corn Laws and their subsequent repeal. This could have been difficult for him. A Liberal, and in close touch with reformers such as Richard Cobden and John Bright, he would have been very keen on free trade, and keen also that the poor, whose staple diet was bread, should be more able to afford it. Living in the country, though, he must have felt for the farming population, who would suffer from low prices. In the event he went flat out for free trade.

Parliament did not perhaps meet for long periods each year, but outside this he seemed busy, his duties stretching from a captaincy in the Berkshire Cavalry and including attendance at Quarter Sessions, as he was Chairman of the County Bench. This took him regularly to Reading, Cricklade, Abingdon, Swindon and Salisbury.

In 1829 he followed in his father's and his grandfather's footsteps and was appointed Recorder of Salisbury.

William was a generous man, providing sites for schools and churches in Downton, Market Lavington and, particularly, in Folkestone. He was wise enough, though, to insert 'reverter clauses' in many of his deeds of gift.

He was Governor of the French Hospital 'La Providence', following again in his father's footsteps. This particular post never passes automatically from father to son. The Governor has to be elected in the first instance, and re-elected or not every third year. His governorship covered an awkward time, when the hospital was moving from Finsbury to Hackney.

In Parliament he never reached high office, but as a back-bencher, he played a prominent and important role. He was, in fact, of enough importance for Palmerston to offer him the Garter. He refused this because of his age, but was hugely pleased that the offer had been made. He is said to have worn the Garter ribbon in his bedcap.

He spent more time at Coleshill than he did at Longford. If there were matters that he had to attend to in Salisbury, he would ride there on horseback, starting at about 6.00 a.m.

At Coleshill he became Master of the Foxhounds, but he gave this up after two years, admitting he was not very good at it. At Longford he contemplated completing Wyatt's work, but, probably wisely, decided it would be too expensive for him to undertake.

William was a great traveller and he would go all over England and into Scotland often accompanied by his two sons.

He travelled on the Continent with the Reverend Charles Woodward in 1833. In 1836 the Court of Copenhagen permitted him and his servants to travel to Sweden. 1851 witnessed him travelling mostly in France. Letters from him in this year from Caen, Dijon, Rouen, Rennes, Nantes, Strasbourg, Geneva and Orleans are still held at Longford and testify to the huge scope of his journeys.

When Viscount Folkestone, Jac, was old enough, William installed him in Longford (1840). He himself, though, looked after Longford well, cleaning some one hundred and six pictures, carrying out repairs, and building new stables.

Jacob was to inherit, but Edward was equally if not more interesting. His career fits more comfortably in the final chapter of this book.

Towards the end William's health deteriorated. He died in 1869 and is buried at Britford.

He was politician, improver, landowner (much was accomplished at Folkestone as well as on the country estates), sportsman and much loved family man. He must rank as possibly the most important and endearing member of the family covered by this brief history.

*William, 3rd Earl of Radnor (in age)*
(Eden Upton Eddis)

71

*Jacob, 4th Earl of Radnor*
(George Richmond)

# CHAPTER X

## *Jacob, 4th Earl of Radnor 1815-1889*

Jacob, or 'Jac', as he was called by friends and family, was born in Portman Square, and lived to a ripe old age. Unlike his brother Edward, who was always referred to as 'Ned', Jac's interests lay almost entirely in the country, in local affairs both lay and Church.

His brother Edward, on the other hand, was a Member of Parliament for a long while, held minor office and became Palmerston's 'precis' writer. In his parliamentary career he suffered a major disappointment. He wished to be Speaker of the House, but was narrowly defeated by another.

It will be remembered that the third Earl travelled to Scotland with some of his children. Perhaps as a result of this, Edward not only married a Balfour of Balbirnie, but also became Member of Parliament for the constituency of Kilmarnock.

Jac's accomplishments were quite different. At school he particularly enjoyed football, gymnastics and dancing. In later life he enjoyed physical work in the country – gardening, all the various skills of farming, not excluding butter and cheese making. He enjoyed, too, carpentry and working with metal.

So far as sport was concerned, he probably enjoyed hunting more than any other, but he fished and shot and swam.

The game books at Longford record this fact. Trout, pike and enormous quantities of grayling were landed and on occasion dispatched to London for some dinner-party or other.

Two of his sports nearly meet on a map of Great Yews at Longford. On the eastern side of the wood are the fox pens, whilst the pheasant pens are on the western side.

He rode to hounds regularly in the New Forest, although he probably forsook that pack in 1869 when he borrowed country from the New Forest, the Portman and the South and West Wilts Hunts to form his own country. The pack was to be known for a while as 'Lord Radnor's'. It subsequently became the Wilton Hunt. The original hounds were bought at Rugby market for £1 each.

Jac's sister, Jane, became known to Queen Victoria through the Duchess of Kent, whom she had first met with her parents, when they were staying in Ramsgate. When the Queen married, Jane was one of her bridesmaids.

The coincidence was that Jac was to marry Mary Frederica Augusta Grimston, who was also a bridesmaid. They married in the same year as the Royal wedding.

In this volume the portrait of Mary Frederica Augusta depicts her in her bridesmaid's dress. At Longford there are two souvenirs of the Queen's wedding. The first is the present that the Queen's bridesmaids were given, whilst the second is a substantial wedge of her wedding cake. The present is an ugly brooch in the form of an eagle made of semi-precious stones. The cake has passed its shelf life but still looks good, and was exhibited last century in an exhibition honouring the memory of Prince Albert.

Jac and Mary produced a large family of seven boys and four girls.

The fourth Earl preferred Longford to Coleshill, and encouraged his second son, Duncombe, to enjoy the latter. When Jac died he left a very comprehensive will with many codicils, the last of which left Coleshill to his second son, his heirs and successors, and so the joining of the two estates occasioned on the death of Sir Mark Pleydell was over. No longer would the Earls of Radnor have to decide how much time they spent on each estate.

At the end of the day most, if not all, of the furniture was sold, and the house itself was bought by a philanthropist, who intended to give it to the National Trust. Whilst refurbishment was progressing towards this end, a carelessly placed blow-lamp ignited the house, and it burnt to the ground. So disappeared one of England's most beautiful houses.

Most of the family portraiture had been returned to Longford before the sale,

*Lady Mary Augusta Frederica Grimston, wife of Jacob, 4th Earl of Radnor*
(Frederick Percy Graves)

and more was to follow in 1985, when the final descendant of Duncombe Pleydell-Bouverie died.

One wall was left standing after the fire. Immured in the wall behind only one course of bricks was the family ghost, a stillborn child embalmed in wax. She did not melt, and, in due course, was returned like the pictures to Longford.

The fourth Earl's third son is worthy of note. He took Holy Orders in Worcester at twenty-two and spent most of his working life as Rector of Pewsey. His wife, too, was of a religious bent, being the daughter of the then Lord Nelson and a member of the Diocesan Synod of Salisbury.

Bertram was a good Rector. He is, though, more famous for his embellishment of Pewsey Church than anything else. He carved the font and sculpted the pulpit. He made and carved the altar rail. Most unusually, and probably quite wrongly, he renewed the roof timbers with timbers taken from the ancient Priory of Ivychurch in Alderbury. At the same time the Nelsons came up with some wood from a French ship, or so they said.

Most famous of all though was his fresco of pink and possibly naked angels. They were almost life size and the last one to be painted was the possessor of two left feet.

In the late twentieth century they were blotted out as being vulgar and unsuitable.

He is said to have run a soup kitchen for the poor and needy, but if he found out that anyone had broken the commandment relating to adultery, then they received no soup until they mended their ways.

The fourth Earl's great work was to join Longford together again. The daunting task was undertaken by Salvin, and the changes he made were massive. A second courtyard was formed and the central one domed over. The south elevation was altered and a low flat and a square tower were employed to finish the task. The architectural work inevitably led to considerable interior decoration, but all in all a good job was done.

Whilst all this was going on, greenhouses were being built in the kitchen garden, and stables as well. These were to be nearer the house than previously.

He had other 'improvements' in mind. Not all of them were effected.

His gardener Ward bred a melon, which is now the traditional engagement present in Japan. They change hands at £100 each.

At one stage of his sporting career Jac attended a hunt meeting where he came under heavy criticism for using bad language in the hunting field. The complaints were so loud and persistent that he was in danger of being asked to resign as Master.

An ancient member of the committee, who had dropped asleep at the back of the hall, suddenly woke up, and getting the gist of the debate, intervened to say 'Of course, Lord Radnor swears. He swears at everybody. He browns the covey and then he is sure of getting his man.'

This then put an end to any serious criticism. He was, in fact, both a good and popular Master of a pack that was of his own creation.

Jac had a good life and a long one. The political stage was not for him. Nor was the business stage. One cannot help but feel he did just what pleased him most, and made a good job of that.

*Edward Pleydell-Bouverie*
*(a cartoon from Vanity Fair)*

# *Epilogue*

This tale purposely ends at the death of the fourth Earl. The fifth Earl's wife, Helen Matilda Chaplin, wrote *From a Great Grandmother's armchair*, which carries the family history forward to 1927 and my own birth.

The family are still occupying most of the Castle. Good pictures, but not all of them, still hang on the walls. There are Pleydell-Bouveries all over the world. I feel quite sure they are as talented as 'the giants of old'. It is the challenge of life that is different.

On a more personal note the author sat in the House of Lords for thirty-one years, being able to bring to that Chamber a practical knowledge of farming, fish-farming, forestry and environmental matters – as well as being able to champion such diverse causes as special education (dyslexia), South America and sea fisheries.

He has the honour too of being the current Governor of the French Hospital, 'La Providence'.

The Castle itself still provides a happy home in which to live. In the 1914–18 War it was a hospital. In the 1939–45 War it was occupied by British and American troops, entertaining such eminent generals as Montgomery[1], Mark Clark[2] and Creagh[3].

[1] Prior to his command of the 8th Army in Africa and of British and Commonwealth forces in Europe.
[2] Established the first American army headquarters in England at Longford in 1942.
[3] Commanded 7th Armoured Division (Desert Rats) in Libya; at Longford for D-Day planning.

LEFT *Longford Castle 1999*

Since the War it has been a focus point for the family. More recently has been added in a South American element.

After the sad conflict of 1982, the first and unofficial face-to-face meeting between the citizens of the Falkland Islands and those of the Argentine Republic was held here in 1996, and everybody got on surprisingly well. Such is the magic of the place.

*'Health and Prosperity*
*Peace and Posterity*
*Long Life and Felicity*
*And the Joys of Eternity'*

BOUVERIE
FAMILY TOAST

LAURENS DES BOUVER[IE]
?(1536-161[ ])
fled to Sandwich 15[ ]
settled at Canterbu[ry]
then London. Silk-Cloth Tra[de]

SAMUEL = Eliz. Forterie
d. before 1621    d. 1625
Silk-Cloth
Trade

JACOB = (1) Eliz. de Fourmestraux
b. Canterbury = (2) Marie Gaillet.
1585-1643  = (3) Catherine
le Truillier
no children

EDWARD = Mary Fourmestraux
1588-1625    d. Canterbury 1631
Merchant    m. at Threadneedle St.
bd St Benet Fink

SAMUEL          PETER = Anne Forterie    Eliz.
JAMES                                    Mary
David    ⎫ all died              Catherine
John     ⎬ 1625.
Henry    ⎭ Plague Year

JACOB    Lea    JAN

DANIEL = Catherine
1629-1703    Hatterieu
Merchant    no children
Des Bouverie
Agent
at Amsterdam

Abraham = Marie
d l'Eau    bapt.
London    Threadneedle
Merchant    St. 1617
Issue

James = Eliz.
Gough    bapt.
Leather    1619
seller
Issue

(1682)
Mary Edwards (1) = Sir WILLIAM
dau. of Alderman    Des Bouverie Bart
Edwards    1656-1717
Merchant
Appointed Governor of
Bank of England (1707)
Knighted (1713)
Created Baronet (1713/4)

(1686)
= (2) Anne Urry
Sole Heiress
of David Urry

EDWARD
b. 1658
d.1673 at
Caen

JACOB
1659-1722
Merchant, Agent
at Aleppo
Bought Honour
and Lordship of
Folkestone and
Terlingham

PETER
1660-82
Merchant, Agent
at Constantinople
d. and bd. there

DANIEL
1667-69
d. London

JOHN
1669-99
Merchant, Agen[t]
at Aleppo
d. at sea
bd. in Cyprus

Edward
baptised Aug.
1683
d. in infancy

Died young
Ann 1687-91
Jacob 1691-92
Ann 1693-1703
John 1695-99
Christopher 1697-98
John 1701-before
1703

(1718)
Sir EDWARD = Mary Smith
2nd Baronet    d. 1721
1688-1736    without issue
Merchant
Bought Longford
Castle (1717)
d. in Aix-la-Chapelle

WILLIAM
1690-1709
Merchant
d. Constantinople

Mary Clarke (1) = Sir JACOB
d. 1739    3rd Baronet
bd. at Britford    1694-1761
1st Viscount
Folkestone and
Baron of
Longford (1747)
Assumed name
BOUVERIE

= (2) Hon. Elizabeth
Marsham
Eldest dau. of
Baron Romney

Died young
Mary 1726-27
Jacob 1727-30/1
Bartholomew
1728-40/1
Harriot 1730-31
Edward
1733/4-34/5

(1747/8)
Harriot Pleydell (1) = WILLIAM
dau. of Sir Mark Pleydell    2nd Viscount Folkestone
d. 1750    1724/5-1776
created Baron Pleydell-
Bouverie and 1st Earl of
Radnor (1765)

(1751)
= (2) Rebecca Alleyne
dau. of John Alleyne
of Four Hills, Barbados
d. 1764

(1765)
= (3) Anne Hales
Dowager Countess
of Feversham

Hon Rev. G. Talbot DD = Ann
Vicar of Guiting    1729-1813
d. 1785
Issue

Anthony = Mary
Ashley Cooper    1730-18[ ]
4th Earl of
Shaftesbury
Issue

Daughter
d. an infant

(1777)
JACOB = Anne Duncombe
2nd Earl of Radnor    step-dau. of Anne,
1749/50-1828    Lady Feversham

WILLIAM HENRY = Lady Bridget
1752-1806    Douglas
dau. of 14th Earl
of Morton
Issue

BARTHOLOMEW = Mary Wyndham
1753-1835    dau. of Hon James
Everard Arundell of
Berwick St John, Wilts
Issue

Catherine (1) = WILLIAM
Pelham-Clinton    3rd Earl of Radnor
1779-1869

= (2) Judith Ann
dau. of Sir Henry Paulet
St. John Mildmay

DUNCOMBE = Louisa May
1780-1850    dau. of Joseph May
Admiral    of Hale lived at
Cliffe Hall,
Lavington, Wilts
Issue

LAURENCE
1781-1811
Called to Bar
d. of consumption
at Clifton
unmarried

General Edward = Catherine
P. Buckley of    1801-75
New Hall,
Wilts

Frances Anne
b. & d. 1804

JACOB = Lady Mary Augusta
4th Earl of Radnor    Frederica Grimston
1815-89    Third dau. of James Walter
1st Earl of Verulam and
Charlotte, dau. of 1st Earl of
Liverpool

EDWARD = Elizabeth Anne
(Ned)    dau. of General Robert
1818-89    Balfour of Balbirnie
MP for Kilmarnock    Inherited Market
Lavington (1869)

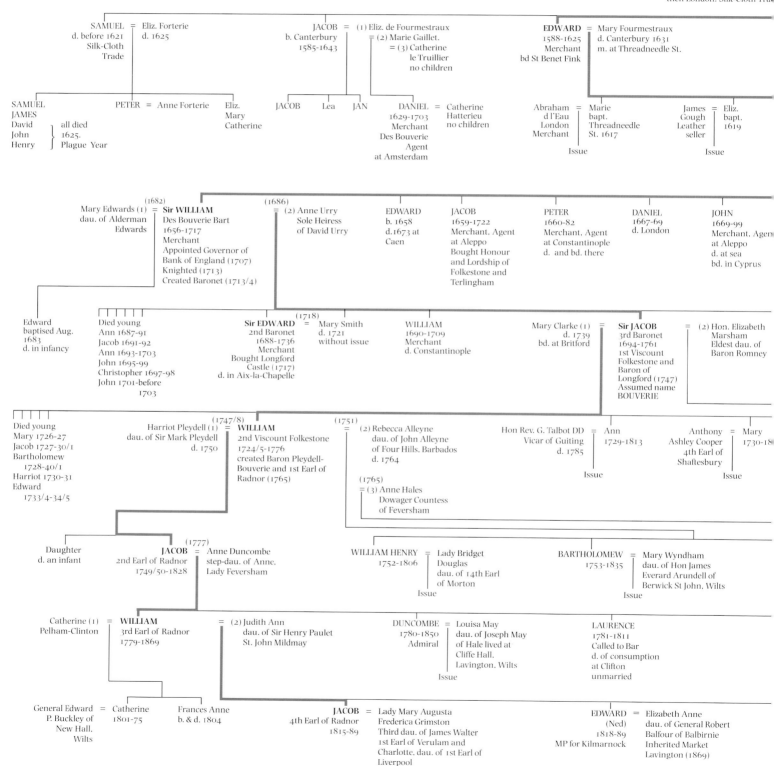

(1) Barbara Van Nynove. d. Canterbury 1591
= (2) Catherine Pipelart at Canterbury 1594
    Widow of Michel Castell
    no children

JOHN d. before
1610

Elias Maurois = Elisabeth
m. Canterbury  b. Sandwich
1593/4

Thomas de la Tombe = Jeanne
Silk Merchant  b. Canterbury
Norwich
m. at Canterbury 1604

Pierre de la Forterie = Lea
Merchant  b. Canterbury
Family from Lille
settled Canterbury 1567

r EDWARD = Anne Forterie
1621-94  1636-77
Knighted  m. Threadneedle
1684/5  St.
Merchant

Nicholas = Jeanne
Adye of  b. 1624
Doddington,
Kent

Issue

Issue

Issue

Issue

Issue

Sir CHRISTOPHER = Elizabeth Freeman
1671-1732/3  of Betchworth, Surrey
Merchant, Agent
at Aleppo
One of the first Directors
of the South Sea Company
Knighted (1713)

John de l'Eau = Jane
of Kensington  1662-81
No issue

Sir Philip = Anne
Boteler of  1663-1717
Teston, Kent

Philip
b. 1695

Mary
1666-89
d. at
Tonbridge

Elizabeth
1673-79
d. at
Greenwich

CHRISTOPHER
1689-1719
Apprentice
Merchant
d. in Cyprus

John = Jane
Allen-Pusey  1700-42

Anne
1704-61
unmarried

FREEMAN
1714-34

JOHN
1722-50
Collector
toured Europe with
James Dawkins and
Rob. Woods
bd. Smyrna

Elizabeth

Daughters

John Grant = Charlotte
of White  1632-1809
Waltham

Sir James Tilney = Harriot
Long. Bart of  1736-77
Draycot Cerne,
Wilts

EDWARD = Harriot
1738-1810  Only dau. of Sir
Edward Fawkener
who inherited
Delapré Abbey

Jacob
1742-44/5

PHILIP = Lucy
BOUVERIE-PUSEY  Eldest dau. of
1746-1828  Robert 4th Earl
Acquired possession of  of Harborough
Pusey Estates

Issue

Issue

EDWARD  (1782)  = (1) Lady Catherine Murray
1760-1824  dau. of John 4th Earl of
Dunmore

Mary Harriot   Harriot Mary
twins, d. 1755
in infancy

Mary Elizabeth   Caroline
d. 1767  1771-72
an infant

FREDERICK = Elizabeth
1785-1857  dau. of Sir Richard
Rector of Hambledon,  Joseph Sullivan Bart
-rey and Pewsey, Wilts
Canon of Salisbury

PHILIP = Marie
1788-1872  dau. of Sir William
Clerk in Bank of  Pierce à Court, Bart
Bosanquet & Co.
d. at Cliffe Hall
Lavington, Wilts

Daughters
d. young

Issue

Issue

Anna Maria
1817-25

William Ellice = Jane Harriet
Second son of William  1819-1903
Ellice of Logie Castle

Sir James Plaisted Wilde = Mary
Baron Penzance  1825-1900

# Index

*As each chapter relates to the sequential inheritors, whose names and relations are shown in the preceding family tree, it has not seemed necessary to repeat these names in the index.*